ANIMAL ADVENTURES
True Stories For The Young and Old
Includes Glossary of Key Terms

BOOTS

Hurricane Katrina Survivor
and Kitten Nanny

Susan J. Juergensen

Story Edited By
Shelley Gillespie

Illustrations By
Dave Grimm

Copyright © 2015 by Susan J. Juergensen

Published and Distributed by ANIMAL ADVENTURES™
An Imprint of Richer Life, LLC
4600 E. Washington Street, Suite 300, Phoenix, Arizona 85034
www.richerlifellc.com

Cover Design: Richer Media USA

Cover Photograph: Courtesy of the Arizona Humane Society®

Illustrations: Dave Grimm

Story Editor: Shelley Gillespie

No part of this publication may be reproduced, stored in a retrieval system, or transmitted in any form or by any means, electronic, mechanical, photocopying, recording, scanning, or otherwise, except as permitted under Section 107 or 108 of the 1976 United States   Copyright Act, without prior written permission of the publisher.

Library of Congress Cataloging-in-Publications Data
2015934170

Susan J. Juergensen

BOOTS
Hurricane Katrina Survivor and Kitten Nanny

ISBN 978-0-9863544-3-4

1. Short Stories 2. Education 3. Non-Fiction

ISBN 13: 978-0-9863544-3-4
ISBN 10: 0986354434

First Edition, March 2015

Printed in the United States of America

ANIMAL ADVENTURES™
An Imprint of Richer Life, LLC

Through its publishing arm, RICHER Press, Richer Life, LLC operates as a full service Trade publisher whose sole goal is to *shape thoughts and change lives for the better.* All of the books, eBooks and digital media we publish, distribute and market embrace our commitment to help maximize opportunities for personal growth and professional achievement.

To learn more visit

www.richerlifellc.com

ANIMAL ADVENTURES
True Stories For The Young and Old

About Animal Adventures

Animal Adventures™ is a series of printed books and eBooks featuring selected "true" short stories. The original manuscripts are written by pet owners who believe that they have inspirational & educational stories about their pets.

All final manuscripts are professionally edited to enhance the entertaining and insightful stories. Each book includes a Glossary of Terms derived from the storyline and custom "caricature" illustrations based on author photographs. These unique features, in a small book format, are intended to enhance the reading enjoyment, educational value and the story's comprehension by young and older readers alike.

If you are a pet owner and have a special story about your pet that you feel would have inspirational and educational value to others, send the Publisher a note at Pets@richerlifellc.com.

About the Story Editor

Shelley Gillespie is an Award-winning journalist, writer speaker, educator, trainer, marketing and writing consultant. She is the founder of Book Writing Success Coach. Book Writing Success Coach offers writing tips expert guidance and personalized coaching to either first time writers who need a coach for direction or experienced writers who need a coach to meet their deadline. As a writing consultant, Shelley has provided inspired copy that helped people win significant clients and business. Shelley is the author of *10 Steps to Book Writing Success*.

About the Illustrator

Dave Grimm is a gifted artist and illustrator. He has been working at his craft for over 30 years. One of Dave's specialties is working with color pencil. He has a natural ability to bring to life some of the most adoring characters and beautiful settings imaginable. Dave's nationally recognized work includes the *Mommy Tell me a Story* children's book series, the *Grandma Annie's Stories From the Garden*™ children's book series and a special children's book co-authored by his wife, Kristi Grimm, and Celebrity Chef and Global Diabetes Advocate, Charles Mattocks, titled *Diabetes and Healthy Eating*.

Acknowledgements

Thanks to my husband, supporters and friends who have endured my huge passion to volunteer and to write.

Special thanks to Arizona Humane Society® staff members and all of the volunteers. You all do amazing work.

Thanks to all of you who volunteer in your community. You do make a difference.

Dedication

This story is dedicated to my grandmother, Opal Inez Pogue, the one who instilled in me the importance of volunteering.

ANIMAL ADVENTURES
True Stories For The Young and Old

MY NAME IS BOOTS

My name is Boots. This name was given to me by some very compassionate people.

You see, I am a Hurricane Katrina survivor. Some of you may not know what that means. Well, it's a weather event that happened in New Orleans, Louisiana…and it changed my life forever.

I remember my family, friends and neighbors all being worried as the hurricane arrived and the wind and the rain came barreling in. Hurricane Katrina blew over trees and street signs and completely flooded the streets of New Orleans when the levies protecting the city from flooding broke. Before I knew what was happening everything was under water! Soccer fields and baseball fields, playgrounds --- and my home!

ANIMAL ADVENTURES
True Stories For The Young and Old

HURRICANE KATRINA

When Hurricane Katrina arrived, people had to evacuate their homes quickly and didn't have time to take many things with them… including their family pets.

I watched my family being rescued with a look of worry on their faces because they had to leave me behind. You see at that time, people were not allowed to take their animals with them to the people shelter. Most of us were left behind.

Being a dog who loved adventure, I knew I would be okay. I knew as bad as this storm was help would soon be on the way. As the days turned into nights, I could hear other dogs barking and cats meowing in the trees. This is how we comforted and kept each other company.

Then, just when we were about to give up, we saw humans! We had not seen people in a long time. They looked so strong and we sensed their compassion for us. They were walking tall, looking all around with clean water and treats. And, they were there to rescue us!

My feet hurt so badly I made my way to them with each step hurting more and more. Suddenly, I saw arms reach out for me, gently picking me up.

"Hey, buddy, looks like you need some help. Come with us!"

The streets were flooded from the hurricane and the only way to rescue us was by boat, so my new friends carefully lifted me onto the boat and we all floated down the street. The team of four rescuers wore dark blue uniforms. I found out later that they were from the Arizona Humane Society®. They were a special team of animal paramedics called Animal Medical Technicians that had traveled all the way to Louisiana to help rescue animals!

I looked around not knowing if I would see my family and neighborhood again, but somehow I knew it was going to be okay. They took me to the animal technician's rescue camp where veterinarians were helping other animals injured in the hurricane. Then they placed me on a surgical table and began repairing my injured feet.

ANIMAL ADVENTURES
True Stories For The Young and Old

EATING AND SLEEPING

The next few days I ate and slept a lot. When they would change my bandages, I always gave kisses to show how thankful I was and also because I felt better. As the days went by, my rescue team had to go back for what they call R&R (Rest and Relaxation) in Arizona, but a new team came to take their place.

I met a woman rescuer who had also been on team number one when the hurricane first hit. This was her second tour.

She looked at me and said "What a sweet face!"

When she asked about my condition, the veterinarian technician told her that it would take time for my feet to heal and that I would need surgery to make sure that my feet did not become infected.

I noticed the same lady would come to check on me and bring me snacks of MREs (Meals-Ready-to-Eat) and take me on potty breaks. I made sure to stick with her because MREs are a lot better tasting than dog food. Soon we were told we could move to the FEMA (Federal Emergency Management Agency) compound. It was where the New Orleans Saints (my team) would practice. All around me were men and women loading and unloading supplies.

A few seconds later, I got a whiff of the air. WOO HOO—chicken and beef! I let my team know I was having what they were having from now on!

A few days later, we were ordered to get out of our semi-truck and trailer and sent to a funny shaped building. I heard someone say it would hold up to an F5 tornado.

ANIMAL ADVENTURES
True Stories For The Young and Old

HURRICANE RITA

That night as we tried to sleep, we had another visitor - Hurricane Rita. Another hurricane! While it wasn't as bad as Hurricane Katrina, it caused some damage. What did that mean for me? Well, because the ground was so wet—and my feet were still healing—I was back to wearing sandwich and bread bags on my feet to go potty. I was so hoping not to have to tell that part. Yes, I was the only dog that had to do this.

Days later, I had a new veterinarian. I called him "fish" because he loved to tell fish tales. Fish and his sidekick took great care of me while my best hurricane buddy went out to work. I sure missed her when she was gone.

Then, one day when she came to see me, she was crying. I heard her say her dog, Ladybug, had collapsed and was in the hospital. Ladybug was back in Arizona, where my new buddy lived, and she was here in New Orleans—far, far away. To comfort her, I kept my head in her lap every time I could and for as long as I could.

Days later she told me her tour in New Orleans was ending and she had to go back to Arizona for R&R and to check on Ladybug. I saw in her eyes the look I call worry. She said if I get to come to Arizona she would take care of me - if I got along with her cat LaLa. Now that was something for me to think about.

The days without her were different. I did not have the same person to use as a pillow every night. However, I was getting better and I was safe. It was then that I heard someone say that Ladybug, my friend's dog, had passed away while she was on the airplane flight back home to Arizona. That made me very sad and I worried about my friend.

ANIMAL ADVENTURES
True Stories For The Young and Old

THE RV CAMPER

One day an RV camper pulled up and I, along with a few other dogs and cats, were placed in it.

We were told that we were going on a "road trip."

I didn't know what that was, but I tried not to look worried. However, my rescue team could tell that I was worried because they said sometimes I would whimper in my sleep. The road trip went by fast and all the rescuers were happy sharing stories, reading newspapers, and talking on cell phones.

We traveled in the RV camper for a few days and nights.

Then one morning, I heard them say, "We're almost home!"

ANIMAL ADVENTURES
True Stories For The Young and Old

ARIZONA LIVING

This is where my life in Arizona begins. We pulled up to a great big building and I could hear other dogs barking in the distance.

My rescuers said, "We're home! We're back at the animal shelter!" Suddenly, I saw lots more people in those spiffy dark blue uniforms and green hospital scrubs who came out to greet us. I saw hugs all around and everyone was taking pictures of us.

Okay, I'm thinking, here we are in Arizona, but where is my hurricane buddy? I was looking at every face hoping to find her! I felt leash slip over my head and was walked into the animal hospital where lots of new people started looking me over. I was very nervous and growled.

Within minutes, in walked my hurricane buddy. I was so excited that my tail almost wagged off my body. I pulled myself together and tried to be on my best behavior and looked up at her, wondering if she still wanted me to come live with her.

ANIMAL ADVENTURES
True Stories For The Young and Old

AFTER MY PHYSICAL EXAM

After my physical exam, she placed me in a kennel in the hospital, with a bowl of dog food.

I thought, here we go again (I wanted the good stuff, chicken and beef tips, like in New Orleans). Oh, well! I was hungry, so I made sure I ate every last morsel so that she would know I was grateful.

She said good night and I'll see you in the morning with a surprise. Early the next morning I was so excited when she came back to see me. As she placed a new collar around my neck and hooked a leash, I wondered where she was taking me. I thought a walk for a potty break but it was so much better. I was going to her house to meet her husband and family for foster care. I didn't know what that was, but it sounded great because she had a big smile on her face!

So what is foster care, you might ask. Well, it's where you live while you are waiting for a permanent home - or if you are injured, or if you are too young and small to be spayed or neutered.

In the case of Hurricane Katrina, many of us rescued animals lived in foster care waiting to see if our original families could be found so that we could go back to them.

When we arrived at her house, I wanted to run inside to first meet LaLa, but I had to remember that my feet were still injured. As I walked gently to her house, I heard sounds of kittens meowing. I walked past LaLa on the couch and thought, "Wow, that went well."

By now the sounds were becoming louder. So, I went over to sniff them. Oh yes, they were kittens all right, and they had just had dinner. I thought I would make myself useful, so I started cleaning them up. As I licked them, I could see them relaxing and sure enough, when I was done, like magic they were asleep. Yes, they had funny wet hairdos thanks to all that licking, but they were fast asleep.

ANIMAL ADVENTURES
True Stories For The Young and Old

BOOTS THE JUNGLE GYM

Later when they woke up, I became Boots the jungle gym. They climbed all over me, hanging off my ears, jumping off my back and using my tail as a slide! It's a very good thing I was a patient dog. I also wanted to impress my hurricane buddy. All this time LaLa was watching and I was sure we would get along.

Then came the day for surgery to help my feet. One thing about Arizona, it doesn't rain much, so no sandwich or bread bags on my feet to keep them dry. Thank goodness!

Soon after my surgery my hurricane buddy and her husband became my new mom and dad. I was what they called "adopted."

My mom was such a good foster mom that every few weeks a new litter of kittens would come home with her. Sometimes the kittens came with their mom, but most of the time they were orphans. I kind of got the feeling I was meant for this job.

Where were all the kittens coming from? Well, unfortunately, people do not spay or neuter their animals, so they keep having babies. There is a simple little operation that takes a few minutes. It's called "spay" for girl cats and dogs and "neuter" for boy cats and dogs. And when it's done, no more kitties and puppies that don't have a family to care for them!

ANIMAL ADVENTURES
True Stories For The Young and Old

THE KITTEN NANNY

Months turned into years and after all my hard work I now have a nick name "Boots the Kitten Nanny."

I have been all over local and national news and the internet. Also, I've had my first limo ride. People love to hear the story of how I help my mom and dad take care of the foster kittens at home—but I am so good at what I do that I have a second job at the shelter in its brand new Kitten Nursery. A kitten nursery is a place where tiny baby kittens and, sometimes, their moms live until they weigh enough for the spay or neuter surgery so they can be put up for adoption at the animal shelter.

ANIMAL ADVENTURES
True Stories For The Young and Old

Kitten Nursery Job

My kitten nursery job is pretty much the same thing I do at home, but now one day a week I go to the animal shelter.

I would let the nursery kittens climb on me or curl up for a nap—especially the ones that come in without their mommies.

I just go slow and let them come to me when they want to. They learn sometimes adventures can be scary, but also fun.

I am one grateful dog. A lot of good came into my life because of the kindness of the Animal Medical Technicians who saved me.

So I have an invitation for everyone who is reading this book. Find a way that you can make a difference in someone's life—animal or human—and you, too, will feel just as blessed as I do to have a chance to help another. It will change your life and the life of the person or animal you help, forever. And when you do, write and tell me about what you did and how it mattered.

ANIMAL ADVENTURES
True Stories For The Young and Old

You can write to me here:
Bootsthekittennanny@yahoo.com

You can also find me here:
Facebook™ at Boots Nicks Juergensen

Now, go find your way!

Boots the Kitten Nanny

ANIMAL ADVENTURES
True Stories For The Young and Old

ABOUT THE AUTHOR

Susan and Boots

Susan Juergensen is an Indiana native. She now lives in Arizona. Over the past 10 years, Susan and her husband have fostered over 300 kittens, cats, puppies and dogs. They were all either recovering from injury or too young or underweight for adoption.

Susan was among the Arizona Humane Society® volunteers who supported the Hurricane Katrina animal rescue and eventually adopted Boots when he was brought to Arizona and was unable to be re-connected with his owners.

It did not take long to discover that Boots was special and he quickly became a part of their family.

Susan plans to write other short stories about Boots and his adventures. Her motivation is to share with others the importance and joy of pet ownership and volunteering.

According to Susan, *"Providing foster care for all of the rescued pets we brought into our home was important. We were able to give each animal the love and care they needed before finding their new, 'fur-ever' homes."*

ANIMAL ADVENTURES
True Stories For The Young and Old

Glossary of Key Terms
Source: Wikipedia, the free encyclopedia

Adventure

An adventure is an undertaking usually involving danger and unknown risks.

Adoption

An adopted child or animal is someone who has been legally taken by another family to be taken care of as their own.

Animal Hospital

An animal hospital is a special place where a pet's health is the top priority. Animal hospitals are places where Veterinarians treat pets and provide medical care. The services usually include a full range of general, surgical and specialized care.

Animal Shelter

An animal shelter is a facility that houses and disposes of homeless, lost, or abandoned animals; mostly dogs and cats. In the past, such a shelter was more commonly referred to as a dog pound, a term which had its origins in the impoundments of agricultural communities, where stray cattle would be penned up or impounded until claimed by their owners.

Animal Medical Technicians

An Animal Medical Technician is a person who is certified to provide medical help to animals. A technician generally performs diagnoses and helps to prevent or treat any disease, illness, pain, deformity, defect, injury, or other physical, mental, or dental condition of any animal.

Arizona

Arizona is a state in the southwestern region of the United States. It is also part of the Western United States and of the Mountain West states. It is the sixth largest and the 15th most populous of the 50 states. Its capital and largest city is Phoenix. Arizona is one of the Four Corners states. It has borders with New Mexico, Utah, Nevada, California, and Mexico, and one point in common with the southwestern corner of Colorado. Arizona's border with Mexico is 389 miles (626 km) long, on the northern border of the Mexican states of Sonora and Baja California.

Arizona Humane Society®

The Arizona Humane Society® is an organization which serves a critical role in Arizona communities. The Society rescues, heals, adopts and advocates for homeless, sick, injured and abused animals. They do this through collaborative partnerships, affordable community services, emergency rescue and its own medical trauma center. The Society is committed to providing second chances and saving the lives of animals.

"Boots"

Boots is the Chow and German shepherd mix, who was saved by the Arizona Humane Society® (AHS) during their Hurricane Katrina rescue efforts. Boots was adopted by an AHS volunteer. He still frequently visits the organization as a "nanny" for kittens — helping them to socialize and become more adoptable.

Compassionate People

Compassionate people are people who express compassion for others. Compassion is the emotion that one feels in response to the suffering of others that motivates a desire to help.

FEMA

FEMA is the acronym for the Federal Emergency Management Agency. FEMA is an agency of the United States Department of Homeland Security, initially created by Presidential Reorganization Plan No. 3 of 1978 and implemented by two Executive Orders on April 1, 1979.

Flooding

Flooding is a great flowing or overflowing of water especially over land not usually submerged or covered.

Grateful

Being grateful is a feeling or the showing thanks to someone for some helpful act.

Hurricane

A Hurricane is a rapidly rotating storm system. It is best known by strong winds and a spinning arrangement of thunderstorms that produce heavy rain. Depending on its location and strength, this kind of weather system can be referred to by other names such as typhoon, tropical storm, cyclonic storm, tropical depression, and simply cyclone.

Hurricane Katrina

Hurricane Katrina was the eleventh named storm and fifth hurricane of the 2005 Atlantic hurricane season. It was the costliest natural disaster, as well as one of the five deadliest hurricanes, in the history of the United States.

Hurricane Rita

Hurricane Rita was the fourth most intense Atlantic hurricane ever recorded and the most intense tropical cyclone ever observed in the Gulf of Mexico. Part of the record-breaking 2005 Atlantic hurricane season, which included three of the six most intense Atlantic hurricanes ever recorded (along with #1 Wilma and #6 Katrina), Rita was the eighteenth named storm, tenth hurricane, and fifth major hurricane of the 2005 season.

Kennel

A kennel is a structure or shelter for dogs or cats. Used in the plural, the kennels, the term means any building, collection of buildings or a property in which dogs or cats are housed, maintained, and (though not in all cases) bred.

Levee

A levee is an embankment, bank, mound or dam designed to prevent the flooding of a river.

MRE

MRE is a Military acronym which means "Meal, Ready to Eat." A modern MRE generally consists of a main course, bread and spread, a desert, powdered drinks, a condiment package, and a heating element (in case the soldier is interested in a semi-hot meal). Each MRE, when fully consumed, is approximately 2000 calories, the suggested daily caloric per day for an average person.

Nanny

A nanny is a care provider, or mother's helper, who provides care for one or more children in a family as a service.

New Orleans, Louisiana

New Orleans is a major United States port and the largest city and metropolitan area in the state of Louisiana. The population of the city was 343,829 as of the 2010 U.S. Census. The New Orleans metropolitan area had a population of 1,167,764 in 2010 and was the 46th largest in the United States. The city is named after the Duke of Orleans, and strongly influenced by European culture.

Nursery

A nursery is a room or area in a household set apart for the use of the young.

Physical Exam

A physical examination is the evaluation of a body to determine its state of health.

Survivor

A survivor is a person, animal or anything that survives or remains alive or in existence after an event in which others have died or have been lost.

Rescue Animals

A rescue animal is any animal that has been placed in a new home after being abused, neglected, or abandoned by its previous owner.

Rescue Team

A Rescue Team is a group of people that conduct search and rescue missions to find someone who may be in trouble. For example, people who may have fallen, gotten lost, or are in troublesome situations.

RV Camper

RV is the acronym for Recreational Vehicles. RVs are either motor vehicles or tow-able trailers and are primarily intended for leisure activities such as vacations and camping. RVs are usually found in RV Parks or campgrounds.

Spay or Neuter Surgery

Spaying or neutering is a surgical procedure to prevent the birth of animal offspring. Female animals are spayed and male animals are neutered. Both procedures are performed while the pet is under general anesthesia and asleep.

Surgical Table

A surgical table is an operating table, sometimes called an operating room table. It is the table on which the patient lies during a surgical operation. This surgical equipment is usually found inside the surgery room of a hospital.

Veterinarians

Veterinarians are doctors who provide medicine and surgery for animals.